SALMON

a cookbook

Colin Simpson

Salmon a cookbook

ISBN-13: 978-1491048337

ISBN-10: 1491048336

DEDICATION

This book is dedicated to my mother, Alice.

Salmon a cookbook

CONTENTS

Grilled Recipes

Stove Top Recipes

Salmon a cookbook

Salmon a cookbook

i

The Author

Dear Friends!

A recent study predicts that by the year 2030, 51% of the US population will be obese. One important way to avoid being part of this statistic is by eating the correct food and living a healthy life style.

Part of a good healthy diet includes eating fish twice week. Salmon is the perfect fish to include in your diet. It is one of the healthiest, leanest and tastiest protein sources. The health benefits of eating Salmon are numerous due to the Omega-3 fatty acids and nutrients found in the fish. Salmon is also power packed with minerals and vitamins.

People new to Salmon are often surprised at what you can do with this delicious tasting fish. My love of Salmon began over 25 years ago at my first job as a cook; my Salmon Chowder became an instant hit. That recipe still gets great reviews from everyone who tries it.

For many years I have shared Salmon recipes with family and friends and I am always asked for more. It really is a great compliment. I wrote this cookbook to share many of my favorite Salmon recipes with you. These great tasting recipes are diverse and simple. It is my hope to encourage you to cook Salmon more often for a healthier you.

Happy healthy cooking,

Colin Simpson

Colin is a professional cook and former restaurateur who resides on the beautiful coast of southern Maine in New England, famous for its seafood. Colin quickly became known for his many Salmon dishes. Salmon Chowder and Salmon Quiche were the most favorite dishes for brunch and dinner.

Acknowledgements

This book would not have been possible without the help and support of my family and friends. Each of them light up my life in many ways, for that I am forever grateful. Rick, my partner and best friend, I could not ask for more. Michael, thank you for all those runs to the local farmer's market. Thank you to Jason, Chris, Brian, BeeJay, Jill, Cheryl and Marisa for all your help and continued support. Maggie, the graphics are wonderful. Dougal, the photographs are beautiful. I love you all.

Introduction

Good organization is key to successful cooking, to avoid mistakes and save time. I have a simple process I use with all recipes which is probably similar to yours, but thought I would share it with you.

After reading the entire recipe through, I ensure all my ingredients and utensils are laid out in place. I pre-heat the oven if required and then do all the prep, following the recipe instructions in the listed order. When ready to cook, I set the timer. Being prepared makes cooking easy, more fun and saves time!

Many of the recipes include healthy side dish suggestions, along with the ingredients and cooking directions. Some of the recipes also include images.

Salmon a cookbook

Baked

Salmon Au Gratin

Prep: 15 min – Cook: 60 min – Serves Six

Ingredients:

1 lb. Salmon Fillet—skin removed—chopped

2 lb. Potatoes—1/8-inch slices—unpeeled

1 Onion—chopped

1 Garlic Clove—minced

2 Cups Milk—low fat

1-1/4 Cup Cheddar Cheese—low fat—shredded

1/2 Cup Mushrooms—sliced

1/3 Cup Breadcrumbs

1/4 Cup Parmesan Cheese—shredded

3 Tablespoons Butter

1 Tablespoon All-purpose Flour

1 Teaspoon Paprika Pepper

1 Teaspoon Italian Seasoning

1 Teaspoon Salt

1 Teaspoon Ground Black Pepper

Directions:

1. Melt butter in a large saucepan over medium heat and sauté the Onion and Garlic in the saucepan for 2 minutes.

2. Mix 1/4 cup of Milk and Flour in a cup. Add rest of Milk, Salt, Pepper and Italian Seasoning to the saucepan. When Milk is warm, stir in cup mix, keep stirring and cook till sauce thickens.

3. Add the Cheddar and Parmesan Cheese to Sauce, stir till Cheese melts. Remove saucepan from heat.

4. Layer bottom of a 1–1/2 quart casserole dish with 1/2 of the sliced potato, layer all the mushrooms on top of the potato. Layer the chopped Salmon evenly over mushrooms, then cover Salmon with remaining potato slices.

5. Slowly pour sauce over Potatoes in casserole dish.

6. Put casserole dish in **preheated 375 degree oven** for 60 minutes. Sprinkle Breadcrumbs and Paprika Pepper on top of casserole. Continue to cook for another 20 minutes.

Baked

Salmon with Red Potato Apple & Blueberries

Prep: 15 min – Cook: 25 min – Serves Four

Ingredients:

4 Salmon Fillets—4 ounces each

2 lb. Baby Red Potatoes

2 Apples—cored—cut into wedges

1/2 Cup Blueberries

4 Shallots—thinly sliced

1 Lemon—Sliced

4 Teaspoons Olive Oil

2 Teaspoons Fresh Dill—chopped

Salt and Black Pepper to taste

Directions:

1. Boil Baby Red Potatoes for 10 minutes.

2. Cut 4—18 inch square pieces of baking foil. Lay out foil flat and lightly coat the center with cooking spray.

3. Place 1 piece of Salmon Fillet on each foil square, skin side down, season with Salt and Pepper.

4. Arrange 1/4 of Red Potato, Apple wedges, sliced Shallots and Blueberries around each Salmon Fillet.

5. Top each Fillet Olive Oil, Dill and a slice of Lemon.

6. Fold foil to make a tightly sealed package. Place foil packs on a baking sheet.

7. Put baking sheet in a **preheated 400 degree oven** and bake for 25 minutes or until Salmon flakes easily with a fork.

8. Put foil contents onto serving plates and cover Salmon with juices from foil packs.

9. Serve immediately.

Served with suggestion:

A green salad and whole wheat bread rolls.

Baked

Barbeque Salmon

Prep: 10 min – Cook: 20 min – Serves Four – Marinade: 60 min

Ingredients:

4 Salmon Fillets—4 ounces each

4 Tablespoons Pineapple Juice

2 Tablespoons Lemon Juice

Combine the following ingredients in a small bowl to make BBQ Sauce:

2 Tablespoons Brown Sugar

1 Tablespoon Lemon Rind

4 Teaspoons Chili Powder

1 Teaspoon Ground Cumin

3/4 Teaspoon Ground Cinnamon

1/2 Teaspoon Salt

Directions:

1. Put Salmon, Pineapple Juice and Lemon Juice in a ziploc bag, seal bag with air removed. Refrigerate for 60 minutes.

2. Lightly coat baking dish with cooking spray.

3. Remove Salmon from marinade, discard marinade.

4. Rub small bowl mix on top of Salmon; place coated Salmon in baking dish skin side down.

5. Put baking dish in a **preheated 400 degree oven** for 20 minutes or until Salmon flakes easily with a fork.

6. Serve immediately.

Served with suggestion:

Vegetables and whole wheat bread rolls.

In a skillet add 1 tablespoon of olive oil, 1 cup baby carrots, 1 cup whole green beans, 1 cup yellow wax beans and 1 teaspoon of Italian seasoning. Cook on medium to low heat for 5 minutes or until desired tenderness, stirring every few minutes.

Baked

Salmon Caesar Salad

Prep: 10 min – Cook: 20 min – Serves Four

Ingredients:

4 Salmon Fillets—4 ounces each—skinless

1 1/2 Cups Croutons

1 Cup Caesar Dressing—low fat

1/4 Cup Parmesan Cheese—grated

2 Romaine Lettuce

1 Lemon—cut into 8 wedges

Combine the following ingredients in a small bowl:

1 1/2 Teaspoons Garlic Salt

2 Teaspoons Fresh Parsley—chopped

1 Teaspoon Lemon Pepper Seasoning

Directions:

1. Lightly coat baking dish with cooking spray.

2. Rub small bowl mix on top of Salmon; place coated Salmon in baking dish.

3. Put baking dish in **preheated 400 degree oven** for 20 minutes or until Salmon flakes easily with a fork.

4. Cut Lettuce into bite size pieces and place in large bowl.

5. Add Caesar Dressing, Parmesan Cheese and Croutons to Lettuce. Toss until combined well.

6. Divide Caesar salad evenly on 4 plates.

7. Cut each Salmon Fillet in half. Place 2 halves on top of each plate.

8. Garnish with 2 Lemon Wedges.

9. Serve immediately.

Served with suggestion:

A side dish of sautéed Zucchini and Summer Squash with whole wheat bread rolls.

Slice 3 large Zucchini and 3 large Summer Squash. Cook with 1 tablespoon of Olive Oil and 1/2 teaspoon of Italian Seasoning in a skillet. Cover and cook for 4–5 minutes over medium heat.

Baked

Orange Salmon with Cranberry Compote

Prep: 10 min – Cook: 20 min – Serves Four

Ingredients:

1 lb. Salmon Fillet—skin removed

1/2 Cup White Wine

1 Tablespoon Olive Oil

2 Oranges—one sliced—one cut into wedges.

4 Cloves

1 Star Anise

1 Bay Leaf

Salt and Ground Black Pepper to taste

Combine the following ingredients in a saucepan:

12 oz. Cranberries—fresh

3/4 Cup of Sugar

1/2 Tablespoon Orange Rind—grated

2 Tablespoons Orange Juice

I Tablespoon Orange Liquor

1/2 Teaspoon Lemon Rind—grated

1/4 Teaspoon Vanilla Extract

1/4 Teaspoon Nutmeg

Pinch of Ground Cinnamon

Directions:

1. Rub both sides of Salmon with Olive Oil.

2. Place Salmon in Baking dish. Pour Wine over Salmon. Top the Salmon with Cloves, Star Anise, Bay Leaf and Orange slices. Sprinkle with Salt and Pepper to taste.

3. Put baking dish in **preheated 400 degree oven** for 20 minutes or until Salmon flakes easily with a fork.

4. Combine the Compote ingredients in a saucepan, cook over medium heat for 5 minutes, stirring often. Reduce heat to medium–low; continue cooking 5 additional minutes or until Compote thickens, remember to keep stirring often. Remove from heat when done.

5. Put cooked Salmon on serving platter and top with Cranberry Compote. Garnish with Orange wedges.

6. Serve immediately.

Baked

Baked Salmon with Mustard Dill Sauce

Prep: 15 min – Cook: 20 min – Serves Four

Ingredients:

4 Salmon Fillets—4 ounces each

1 Lemon—cut into wedges

Combine the following ingredients in a small bowl to make Mustard Dill Sauce:

1 Cup Sour Cream—low fat

3 Tablespoons Fresh Dill—chopped

2 Tablespoons Onion—minced

2 Tablespoons Dijon Mustard

1 Tablespoon Lemon Juice

2 Teaspoons Garlic—minced

Salt and Ground Black Pepper

Directions:

1. Make Sauce, put to the side.

2. Lightly coat baking dish with cooking spray.

3. Place Salmon in baking dish, skin side down.

4. Top each Salmon Fillet with 2 tablespoons of Mustard Dill Sauce.

5. Put baking dish in a **preheated 400 degree oven** for 20 minutes or till Salmon flakes easily with a fork.

6. Serve immediately with remainder of sauce on the side. Garnish with Lemon wedges.

Served with suggestion:

Baby red potatoes and bell peppers go well with the mustard dill sauce.

Cut 1 of each; Green, Red, Yellow and Orange Peppers into strips. Dice enough Eggplant to make 1 cup. In a skillet, add 1 tablespoon olive oil, 1 teaspoon Italian seasoning, Pepper strips and cubed Eggplant. Stir fry on medium heat for 4 minutes, or until desired tenderness.

Baked

Salmon Gyro

Prep: 15 min – Cook: 20 min – Serves Four

Ingredients:

4 Salmon Fillets—4 ounces each—skin removed

2 Pita Bread

1/2 Iceberg Lettuce—shredded

2 Tomatoes—sliced

1/2 Red Onion—sliced

2 Teaspoons Old Bay Seasoning

Cooking Spray

Combine the following ingredients in a small bowl to make Sauce:

1 Cup Sour Cream

2/3 Cup Cucumber—peeled—diced

1 Tablespoon Lemon Juice

2 Teaspoons Fresh Dill—chopped

1/2 Teaspoon Garlic—minced

1/2 Teaspoon Dijon Mustard

1/4 Teaspoon Garlic Powder

Salt and Black Pepper to taste

Directions:

1. Make Sauce and put in refrigerator.

2. Lightly coat baking dish with cooking spray.

3. Sprinkle 1/2 teaspoon of Old Bay seasoning on each piece of Salmon. Place Salmon in baking dish.

4. Put baking dish in a **preheated 400 degree oven** for 20 minutes or until Salmon flakes easily with a fork. Remove from oven.

5. Warm Pita in oven for 2 minutes, then cut Pita in half.

6. Place Salmon Fillet in each Pita.

7. Top Salmon with Lettuce, Tomato, Onion and Sauce.

8. Serve immediately.

Baked

Salmon with Leek Zucchini and Carrot

Prep: 15 min – Cook: 25 min – Serves Four

Ingredients:

4 Salmon Fillets—4 ounces each

2 Leeks—cut into strips

2 Zucchini—cut into strips

4 Carrots—cut into strips

2 Lemons—1 juiced—1 sliced

1 Tablespoon Fresh Parsley—chopped

4 Teaspoons Olive Oil

1 Teaspoon Old Bay Seasoning

Salt and Ground Black Pepper to taste

Directions:

1. Cut 4—18 inch square pieces of baking foil. Lay out foil flat and lightly coat the center with cooking spray.

2. Place 1 piece of Salmon Fillet on each foil square, skin side down.

3. Arrange the Zucchini, Carrots and Leeks around each Salmon Fillet. Sprinkle Old Bay Seasoning on top.

4. Top each fillet with Lemon Juice, 1 teaspoon Olive oil, Parsley, Lemon Slice, Salt and Pepper to taste.

5. Fold foil to make a tightly sealed package. Place foil packs on a baking sheet.

6. Put baking sheet in a **preheated 400 degree oven** for 25 minutes or until Salmon flakes easily with a fork.

7. Put foil contents onto serving plates and cover Salmon with juices from foil pack.

Served with suggestion:

Boil red potatoes with a few mint leaves. A green salad and whole wheat bread rolls.

Baked

Salmon with Maple Orange Thyme

Prep: 10 min – Cook: 20 min – Serves Four

Ingredients:

4 Salmon Fillets—4 ounces each

1 Tablespoon Olive Oil

Combine the following ingredients in a small bowl:

1/2 Cup Orange Juice

2 Teaspoons Orange Zest

2 Teaspoons fresh Thyme—chopped

1 Tablespoon Maple Syrup

Pinch of Ground Black Pepper

Directions:

1. Lightly coat baking dish with cooking spray.

2. Place Salmon in baking dish, skin side down.

3. Top each Salmon Fillet with bowl mix.

4. Put baking dish in a **preheated 400 degree oven** for 20 minutes or till Salmon flakes easily with a fork.

5. Transfer cooked Salmon to serving plates and top with juices from baking dish.

6. Serve immediately.

Served with suggestion:

Boiled red potato and sautéed vegetables complete this healthy dish.

In a skillet, add 1 tablespoon of olive oil, 1 cup baby carrots, 1 cup whole green beans, 1 cup yellow wax beans and 1 teaspoon of Italian seasoning. Cook on medium to low heat for 6 minutes, or until desired tenderness, stirring every few minutes

Baked

Salmon Pasta with Tomato Sauce

Prep: 15 min – Cook: 20 min – Serves Four

Ingredients:

4 Salmon Fillets—4 ounces each—skin removed

8 oz. Spaghetti—cooked

4 Tomatoes—diced

1 Red Onion—sliced

1 Red Pepper—diced

1 Garlic Clove—minced

3 Tablespoons Lemon Juice

2 Tablespoons Honey

1 Tablespoon Olive Oil

1 Tablespoon Fresh Parsley—chopped

1 Teaspoon Italian Seasoning

Ground Black Pepper to taste

Directions:

1. Cook Spaghetti al dente per package directions.

2. Lightly coat baking dish with cooking spray.

3. Place Salmon in baking dish.

4. Brush Salmon Fillet with Honey, sprinkle with Italian Seasoning and Black Pepper to taste.

5. Put baking dish in a **preheated 400 degree oven** for 20 minutes or till Salmon flakes easily with a fork.

6. Put Olive Oil in a skillet on medium heat; add Garlic, Onion and Red Pepper. Sauté for 5 minutes.

7. Add Tomato to skillet, cook another 2 minutes. Remove from heat.

8. Add cooked Spaghetti and Lemon Juice to skillet, stir.

9. Place Spaghetti on serving plates. Place Salmon Fillet on top of pasta. Sprinkle with fresh chopped Parsley.

10. Serve immediately.

Served with suggestion:

A green salad and whole wheat bread rolls.

Baked

Smoked Salmon Pate

Prep: 15 min – Cook: 20 min – Serves Four – Cooling: 120 min

Ingredients:

8 oz. Salmon Fillet—skin removed

1 Cup Cream Cheese—low fat

1/4 Cup Cashew Nuts—finely chopped

1 Tablespoon Onion— chopped

1 Tablespoon Fresh Parsley—chopped

1 Tablespoon Fresh Chives—chopped

1 Tablespoon Fresh Dill—chopped

1 Tablespoon Lemon Juice

1/2 Teaspoon Liquid Smoke*

1/4 Teaspoon Cayenne Pepper

Directions:

1. Lightly coat baking dish with cooking spray, put Salmon in baking dish, and sprinkle Salmon with Paprika Pepper.

2. Put baking dish in **preheated 400 degree oven** for 20 minutes or till Salmon flakes easily with a fork.

3. Remove Salmon from baking dish to a plate. Put to the side and allow cooling.

4. In your food processor combine the cooled Salmon, Cream Cheese, Onion, Lemon Juice, Liquid Smoke and Cayenne Pepper till smooth.

5. Place Smoked Salmon Pâté into 4 small serving dishes, cover and refrigerate for 2 hours**.

6. Sprinkle with chopped Herbs and Cashews just before serving.

*Liquid Smoke can be omitted if desired to make 'Salmon Pâté'.

**Pâté' can be made up to 24 hours in advance.

Served with suggestion:

Whole wheat toast – toasted bagel – toasted muffin and/or crackers with a green side salad.

Baked

Salmon Red Potato Cucumber Mint Salad

Prep: 15 min – Cook: 20 min – Serves Four

Ingredients:

4 Salmon Fillets—4 ounces each

2 lb. Baby Red Potatoes—cut each potato in 1/2

2 Carrots—cut into thin strips

1 Small Cucumber—cut into thin strips

1 Lemon—Juice Only

1 Teaspoon Lemon Pepper Seasoning

Combine the following ingredients in a small bowl to make Sauce:

1/3 Cup Mayonnaise—low fat

1 Lemon—Juice Only

1-1/2 Tablespoons Mint Leaves—chopped

Black Pepper to taste

Directions:

1. Boil the Red Potatoes till tender. Drain and put Potatoes in large bowl.

2. Combine the Carrot and Cucumber strips with Potatoes and 1/2 the small bowl mix Sauce. Refrigerate.

3. Lightly coat baking dish with cooking spray.

4. Place Salmon in baking dish, skin side down.

5. Sprinkle the top each Salmon Fillet with Lemon Juice, Lemon Seasoning and Pepper to taste.

6. Put baking dish in **preheated 400 degree oven** for 20 minutes or till Salmon flakes easily with a fork.

7. Serve immediately with Potato Salad. Spoon the rest of the Sauce on top of Salmon.

Served With Suggestion:

A green salad and whole wheat bread Rolls, or a side of your favorite green vegetables.

Baked

Salmon Quiche

Prep: 15 min – Cook: 60 min – Serves Six

Ingredients:

8 oz. Salmon Fillet—skin removed—cubed

Nine-inch Pie Crust

4 Eggs—medium

1 1/2 Cups Milk—2% fat

1/2 Cup Cheddar Cheese—low fat—shredded

4 Mushrooms—sliced

1 Onion—medium—chopped

3 Tablespoons Olive Oil

1 Tablespoon Lemon Juice

1 Tablespoon Fresh Dill Weed—chopped

1 Tablespoon Fresh Parsley—chopped

1 Teaspoon Worcestershire Sauce

1 Teaspoon Salt

1/4 Teaspoon Ground Black Pepper

Directions:

1. Put Olive Oil in a saucepan on medium-low heat. Add the Onion and sauté for 3-4 minutes. Add the Lemon Juice, Worcestershire Sauce, sliced Mushrooms and cubed Salmon to the saucepan. Sauté till salmon is cooked, about 5 minutes. Remove from heat. The Salmon will break into smaller pieces as it cooks. Put to the side.

2. In a bowl, combine the Eggs, Milk, Cheese, Parsley, Dill, Salt and Pepper. Put to the side.

3. Put the EMPTY Pie Crust in a **preheated 450 degree** oven for 5 minutes.

4. Remove Pie Crust from Oven. **Turn oven down to 350 degrees**.

5. Combine the cooked Salmon in the bowl mix, stir well. Pour bowl mix into Pie Crust.

6. Put Pie Crust back into oven and cook for 50 minutes.

Served With Suggestion:

Serve with a green salad or fruit salad.

Baked

Salmon with Grapes

Prep: 10 min – Cook: 20 min – Serves Four

Ingredients:

4 Salmon Fillets—4 ounces each—skin removed

1/2 Cup Grape Juice

2 Teaspoons Fresh Dill—chopped

Ground Black Pepper to taste

Combine the following ingredients in a small bowl to make Grape Sauce:

1/2 Cup Grapes—seedless—halved

1/2 Cup Yogurt—low fat

2 Tablespoons Fresh Mint—chopped

Directions:

1. Lightly coat baking dish with cooking spray.

2. Put Salmon in baking dish, pour in Grape Juice, and sprinkle top of Salmon with Dill, season with a Ground Black Pepper. Cover baking dish with foil.

3. Put covered baking dish in **preheated 400 degree oven** for 20 minutes or till Salmon flakes easily with a fork.

4. Make the Grape Sauce; allow to stand at room temperature.

5. Place cooked Salmon on a serving plate.

6. Spoon Grape Sauce over cooked Salmon.

7. Serve immediately.

Served With Suggestion:

Baked potato and your choice of vegetables with a side salad complete this great tasting healthy meal.

Baked

Salmon Melt Sandwich

Prep: 10 min – Cook: 20 min – Serves Four

Ingredients:

4 Salmon Fillets—4 ounces each—skin removed

8 Slices Rye Bread

4 Slices Swiss cheese

2 Tomatoes—sliced

Old Bay seasoning to taste

Combine the following ingredients in a small bowl to make Sauce:

1/4 Cup Mayonnaise—low fat

1/4 Cup Celery—finely chopped

1 1/2 Tablespoons Onion—finely chopped

1 Teaspoon Apple Cider Vinegar

Salt and Black Pepper to taste

Directions:

1. Make the Sauce, put to side when done.

2. Place Salmon in baking dish, lightly sprinkle with Old Bay Seasoning.

3. Put baking dish in **preheated 400 degree oven** for 20 minutes or until Salmon flakes easily with a fork. Put cooked Salmon to the side.

4. Preheat oven broiler.

5. Place the Rye Bread on a baking sheet and broil for 1 minute, then remove from heat. Spread 1 tablespoon of Sauce on each slice of Rye Bread. Put 4 slices to the side.

6. Add a Fillet to the remaining 4 slices of Rye Bread on the baking sheet. Cover Salmon with 2 slices of Tomato and finish with a slice of Cheese of top.

7. Return baking pan to the oven and broil till Cheese melts, and then remove from oven.

8. Cover Melt with last slice of Rye Bread and cut the sandwich diagonally.

9. Serve immediately.

Baked

Salmon Pie

Prep: 20 min – Cook: 40 min – Serves Six

Ingredients:

1 lb. Salmon Fillet—skin removed—chopped

2 lb. Potatoes—diced

1 Cup Mayonnaise—low fat

2 Eggs—hard boiled—sliced

1 Onion—minced

2 Tablespoons Fresh Parsley—chopped

1 Tablespoon Olive Oil

1 Tablespoon Lemon Juice

1 Teaspoon Garlic—minced

1 Teaspoon Paprika

1/2 Teaspoon Salt

1/4 Teaspoon White Pepper

Directions:

1. Boil the Eggs, put to the side and let cool.

2. Boil the Potatoes and mash them. Do not add milk or butter. Add 1 cup of Mayonnaise, Minced Garlic, Paprika, and 1 tablespoon chopped Parsley, Salt and Pepper to the mashed Potato, stir well. Put to the side.

3. Add Olive Oil to a skillet over medium heat, sauté the onions for 2 minutes, and then add the chopped Salmon and Lemon Juice. Continue to sauté till Salmon is cooked, about 4 minutes.

4. Combine the Salmon and Potatoes, mix well.

5. Put Salmon mix in a 9-in pie plate.

6. Put pie plate in **preheated 350 degree oven** for 30 minutes. Remove from oven when done.

7. Top Salmon Pie with sliced Egg and garnish with 1 tablespoon of chopped Parsley.

8. Serve immediately.

Served with suggestion:

Green beans, a side salad and whole wheat bread rolls complete this delicious meal that is sure to satisfy the heartiest appetite.

Baked

Salmon on Red Potato with White Wine Sauce

Prep: 20 min – Cook: 20 min – Serves Four

Ingredients:

4 Salmon Fillets—4 ounces each—skin removed

2 lb. Red Potatoes—mashed

2 Tablespoons Butter

2 Tablespoons Milk—2% fat

2 Tablespoons Fresh Dill—chopped

2 Garlic Cloves—minced

Salt and Black Pepper to taste

Combine the following ingredients in a small skillet:

1/2 Cup White Wine

1/2 Cup Shallots—minced

1/4 Cup White Wine Vinegar

3 Tablespoons Butter

1 Lemon—juiced

White Pepper to taste

Directions:

1. Boil Red Potatoes with skin on, then mash with 2 tablespoons of Butter, 2 tablespoons of Milk and minced Garlic. Add Salt and Pepper to taste.

2. Cut 4—18 inch square pieces of baking foil. Lay out foil flat and lightly coat the center with cooking spray.

3. Divide the Potato into 4 portions. Place one portion of Potato on the center of each piece of foil and flatten to size – slightly larger than Salmon Fillet.

4. Place Salmon Fillet on top of Potato and sprinkle with Dill.

5. Fold foil to make a tightly sealed package. Place foil packs on a baking sheet.

6. Put baking sheet in **preheated 450 degree oven** for 20 minutes.

7. Simmer skillet ingredients till sauce is reduced.

8. Open foil packets and place under broiler to brown top of potato, about 4 minutes, remove Potato from foil and place on plates, and top with sauce. Garnish with Dill.

9. Serve immediately.

Baked

Spiced Salmon with Peppers

Prep: 15 min – Cook: 20 min – Serves Four

Ingredients:

4 Salmon Fillets—4 ounces each

1 Red Pepper—cut into strips

1 Yellow Pepper—cut into strips

1/2 Cup Pineapple Juice

1/2 Cup Orange juice

2 Tablespoons of Olive Oil

Combine the following ingredients in a small bowl:

1 Tablespoon fresh Oregano—chopped

2 Teaspoons Garlic— minced

2 Teaspoons Cumin—ground

3/4 Teaspoon Salt

Directions:

1. Put 1 Tablespoon of Olive Oil in a skillet over medium heat. Add the Pepper strips and sauté for a few minutes till Peppers begin to brown.

2. Add Pineapple Juice, Orange Juice and 2 Teaspoons of small bowl mix to skillet, continue to heat for 2 minutes, stirring a few times. Remove skillet from heat.

3. Lightly coat baking dish with cooking spray.

4. Add 2 Teaspoons of Olive Oil to remainder of small bowl mix, stir to make a paste.

5. Rub small bowl mix on top of Salmon; place coated Salmon in baking dish, skin side down. Pour skillet contents over Salmon.

6. Put baking dish in **preheated 400 degree oven** for 20 minutes or until Salmon flakes easily with a fork.

7. Serve immediately.

Served With Suggestion:

In a skillet add 1 tablespoon of olive oil, 1 cup baby carrots, 1 cup whole green beans, 1 cup yellow wax beans and 1 teaspoon of Italian seasoning. Cook on medium to low heat for 5 minutes or until desired tenderness, stirring every few minutes.

Baked

Whole Baked Salmon with Lime Dressing

Prep: 20 min – Cook: 40 min – Serves Six – Marinade: 30 min

Ingredients:

1 3 lb. Salmon Fillet

1 Lime—juice only

1 Tablespoon Fresh Dill—chopped

Salt and Ground Black Pepper to taste

6 Eggs—hard boiled

10 Capers

1 Cucumber—sliced

Combine the following ingredients in a blender to make Dressing:

2/3 Cup Ketchup

1 Cup Sugar

1 Cup Olive Oil

1/2 Cup Lemon Juice

1 Onion

2 Garlic Cloves

1 Teaspoon Paprika

1 Teaspoon Salt

Pinch of Ground Black Pepper

Directions:

1. Make the Dressing, then refrigerate.

2. Lightly coat large baking dish with cooking spray.

3. Place Salmon in baking dish. Spread Olive Oil and 1 Lime over Salmon, Salt and Pepper to taste. Sprinkle top with Dill.

4. Cover baking dish, put to the side for 30 minutes.

5. Make hard boiled Eggs. Put cooked Eggs in bowl of cold water and refrigerate.

6. Put baking dish in **preheated 300 degree oven** for 60 minutes or until Salmon flakes easily with a fork.

7. Carefully remove Salmon from baking dish to a platter. Remove Egg shells, cut Eggs into quarters and arrange around Salmon with Cucumber slices and Capers. Pour Dressing over Salmon.

8. Serve immediately.

Baked

Salmon Tacos

Prep: 15 min – Cook: 15 min – Serves Six – Marinade: 60 min

Ingredients:

1 lb. Salmon Fillet—skin removed—cut into 1" cubes

1/2 Iceberg Lettuce—shredded

1/2 Cup Sour Cream—low fat

1/2 Cup Guacamole

1/2 Cup Mexican Blend Cheese—low fat—shredded

2 Tomatoes—diced

2 Tablespoons Lime Juice

Salt to taste

8 Flour Tortillas—6 inch

Combine the following ingredients in a small bowl:

2 Tablespoons Lime Juice

1 1/2 Teaspoons Ground Cumin

1 1/2 Teaspoons Garlic Powder

1 Teaspoon Paprika

1 Teaspoon Fresh Oregano—chopped

1/4 Teaspoon Cayenne Pepper

Directions:

1. Prepare small bowl mix then add Salmon cubes, stir to coat Salmon cubes with bowl mix.

2. Put Salmon in baking dish. Cover and refrigerate for 1 to 2 hours.

3. Remove cover from baking dish; sprinkle Salmon with salt to taste. Cover baking dish with foil.

4. Put baking dish in **preheated 375 degree oven** for 15 minutes or until Salmon flakes easily with a fork

5. Combine Sour Cream with 2 tablespoons Lime Juice.

6. Heat Tortillas in oven for 2 minutes after Salmon has cooked.

7. Spoon salmon onto warm Tortillas; add Lettuce, Tomatoes, Cheese, Sour cream and Guacamole.

8. Fold Tortillas to make wrap, serve immediately.

Served with suggestion:

Brown Rice and Black Beans.

Baked

Salmon Wrap

Prep: 15 min – Cook: 20 min – Serves Four

Ingredients:

4 Salmon Fillets—4 ounces each—skin removed

1 teaspoon Paprika Pepper

Salt and Pepper to taste

4 Flour Tortillas

2 tomatoes—large—sliced

1 Cup Lettuce—shredded

Combine the following ingredients in a small bowl to make Sauce:

3 Tablespoons Mayonnaise—low fat

2 Tablespoons Greek Yoghurt—low fat

2 Tablespoon Lemon Juice

1 Teaspoons Dill—fresh, chopped

1 Teaspoon Parsley—fresh, chopped

Salt and Pepper to taste

Directions:

1. Lightly coat baking dish with cooking spray.

2. Put Salmon in baking dish and sprinkle with Paprika and Salt and Pepper to taste.

3. Put baking dish in **preheated 400 degree oven** for 20 minutes, or until Salmon flakes easily with a fork

4. When Salmon is cooked and removed from oven, put Tortillas in oven for 1 minute, enough to warm Tortillas. Remove Tortillas from oven.

5. Lay Tortillas flat and add 1 Salmon Fillet to each one.

6. Spoon Sauce evenly over each piece of Salmon.

7. Sprinkle Lettuce on top of Sauce, and cover with Tomato slices.

8. Fold Tortilla to make warp.

9. Serve immediately.

Served with suggestion:

Potato salad, fruit salad or potato chips on the side.

Baked

Ginger Cinnamon Salmon

Prep: 10 min – Cook: 20 min – Serves Four

Ingredients:

4 Salmon Fillets—4 ounces each—skin removed

1 Lemon—sliced

Combine the following ingredients in a small bowl:

1 Garlic Clove—chopped

2 Teaspoons Olive Oil

1 Teaspoon Lemon Juice

1 Teaspoon Ground Cinnamon

1 Teaspoon Ground Ginger

Salt and Ground Black Pepper to taste

Directions:

1. Lightly coat baking dish with cooking spray.

2. Rub bowl mix over Salmon, put Salmon in baking dish.

3. Cover Salmon with Lemon slices.

4. Put baking dish in **preheated 400 degree oven** for 20 minutes or till Salmon flakes easily with a fork.

Baked

Honey Mustard Salmon Steaks

Prep: 10 min – Cook: 20 min – Serves Four

Ingredients:

4 Salmon Steaks—4 ounces each—skin removed

Combine the following ingredients in a small bowl:

2 Tablespoons Dijon Mustard

2 Teaspoons Honey

1 Teaspoon Fresh Thyme—chopped

Black Pepper to taste

Directions:

1. Lightly coat baking dish with cooking spray.

2. Put Salmon Steaks in baking dish.

3. Spread bowl mix on top of Salmon Steaks.

4. Put baking dish in preheated 400 degree oven for 20 minutes or until Salmon flakes easily with a fork.

5. Serve immediately.

Served with suggestion:

Serve with a baked potato, your favorite vegetable, whole wheat bread rolls and a side salad.

Baked

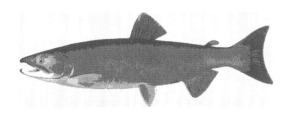

Salmon with Sweet Dill Mustard Sauce

Prep: 10 min – Cook: 20 min – Serves Four

Ingredients:

4 Salmon Fillets—4 ounces each—skin removed

1 Lemon—sliced thin

Combine the following ingredients in a small bowl to make Sauce:

1/3 Cup Olive Oil

1/4 Cup Fresh Dill—chopped

3 Tablespoons Sweet Honey Mustard

1 Tablespoon Dijon Mustard

1 Teaspoon Sugar

Salt and Ground Black Pepper to taste

Directions:

1. Lightly coat baking dish with cooking spray.

2. Put Salmon in baking dish and spoon sauce on top. Place Lemon slices on top of sauce.

3. Put baking dish in **preheated 400 degree oven** for 20 minutes or till Salmon flakes easily with a fork.

4. Serve immediately with your favorite side dish.

Baked

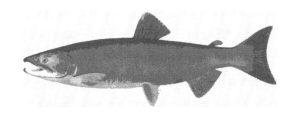

Salmon in White Wine and Lemon Juice

Prep: 10 min – Cook: 20 min – Serves Four – Marinade: 60 min

Ingredients:

4 Salmon Fillets—4 ounces each—skin removed

1–1/2 Cups White Wine

2 Lemons—1 juiced—1 sliced

1 Tablespoon Fresh Dill—chopped

Salt and Ground Black Pepper to taste

Directions:

1. Put the Wine, juice from 1 Lemon, and the Salmon into a ziploc bag, squeeze out the air. Refrigerate for 60 minutes.

2. Lightly coat baking dish with cooking spray.

3. Place Salmon in baking dish, discard marinade.

4. Season Salmon with Salt and Pepper, sprinkle Dried Dill on Salmon and top with Lemon slices.

5. Put baking dish in **preheated 400 degree oven** for 20 minutes or till Salmon flakes easily with a fork.

6. Transfer cooked Salmon to serving plates.

GRILLED RECIPES

Grilled

Orange Maple Glazed Salmon

Prep: 10 min – Cook: 10 min – Serves Four

Ingredients:

4 Salmon Fillets—4 ounces each

Combine the following ingredients in a small bowl to make marinade:

1/3 Cup Orange Juice

1/3 Cup Maple Syrup

3 Tablespoons Apple Cider Vinegar

1 Tablespoon Olive Oil

1 Tablespoon Honey

2 Teaspoons Orange Zest

3 Garlic Cloves—minced

Directions:

1. Make small bowl mix to make marinade, refrigerate for 1 hour.

2. Oil grill and preheat to medium-high.

3. Glaze both sides of Salmon; place glazed Salmon onto hot grill-top side down first.

4. Grill Salmon for 4 minutes on each side—or till Salmon flakes easily with a fork. Brush Salmon with more marinade as it cooks.

5. Serve immediately.

Served With Suggestion:

Grilled zucchini, squash and eggplant and baked potato.

Slice 3/4 inch lengthwise: 3 zucchini, 3 squash and 1 eggplant. In a small bowl combine 2 tablespoons of olive oil, 2 tablespoons apple cider vinegar, 2 teaspoons italian seasoning, 1 minced garlic clove, salt and pepper to taste. Brush vegetables with mix and grill for 5-6 minutes, or until desired tenderness is reached.

Grilled

Asian Style Salmon

Prep: 15 min – Cook: 10 min – Serves Four – Marinade: 60 min

Ingredients:

4 Salmon Fillets—4 ounces each

Combine the following ingredients in a small bowl to make Marinade:

1 Tablespoon Dry Sherry

1 Tablespoon Soy Sauce

1 Tablespoon Sesame Oil

1 Teaspoon Fresh Ginger—minced

1 Garlic Clove—minced

3 Scallions—bulbs only—minced

Salt and Ground Black Pepper to taste

Directions:

1. Combine marinade ingredients in a small bowl.

2. Put Salmon and marinade in a ziploc bag, seal bag with air removed. Refrigerate for 60 minutes.

3. Oil grill and preheat to medium-high.

4. Remove Salmon from marinade.

5. Grill Salmon 4 minutes on each side—or till Salmon flakes easily with a fork.

6. Brush Salmon with more marinade as it cooks.

7. Serve immediately.

Served With Suggestion:

Long grain rice and julienned vegetables complete this dish.

Cut 3 carrots, 3 zucchini and 3 summer squash into 2 inch long thing strips. Heat 1 tablespoon of olive oil in a skillet over medium-high heat. Add julienned vegetables, season with salt and pepper. Sauté for 2-3 minutes or until desired tenderness is reached.

Grilled

Blackened Salmon Sandwich

Prep: 10 min – Cook: 10 min – Serves Four

Ingredients:

4 Salmon Fillets—4 ounces each—remove skin

1 Cup Lettuce—shredded

2 Tomatoes—sliced

1/2 Red Onion—thinly sliced

1 Avocado—pitted

2 Tablespoons Mayonnaise—low fat

2 Teaspoons Cajun Seasoning

4 Whole Wheat Rolls—toasted

Directions:

1. Oil grill and preheat to medium–high.

2. Rub Cajun Seasoning on both side of Salmon. Cook for 3–4 minutes on each side—or till Salmon flakes easily with a fork.

3. Mash Avocado in a small bowl then add Mayonnaise.

4. Split rolls and toast them.

5. Spread Avocado on toasted Rolls, top with Salmon, Lettuce, Tomato and Onion.

6. Serve immediately.

Served with suggestion:

Homemade Red Potato oven fries.

Cut 4 red potatoes into wedges-leave skin on, parboil for 6 minutes. Run wedges under cold water to cool them. Put 1 tablespoon olive oil in a bowl, add wedges, gently stir to coat wedges with oil. Put wedges on baking sheet, sprinkle wedges with a garlic salt. Bake fries in 425 degree preheated oven for 20 minutes, turn wedges over once during baking.

Grilled

Chili Salmon

Prep: 15 min – Cook: 10 min – Serves Four

Ingredients:

4 Salmon Fillets—4 ounces each

1 Tablespoon Olive Oil

Combine the following ingredients in a small bowl:

1 1/2 Teaspoons Chili Powder

1 Teaspoon Brown Sugar

1/2 Teaspoon Cumin

Salt to taste

Directions:

1. Preheat grill to medium heat.

2. Brush Salmon with Olive Oil.

3. Rub small bowl mix into Salmon Steaks.

4. Grill Salmon 4 minutes on each side—or till Salmon flakes easily with a fork.

5. Serve immediately.

Served with suggestion:

Grilled Asparagus Spears and Baked Potato. Coat Asparagus with Olive Oil, sprinkle with kosher salt. Grill the Asparagus Spears turning every few minutes, for 5 minutes, or until desired tenderness is reached.

Grilled

Salmon and Eggplant

Prep: 15 min – Cook: 10 min – Serves Four – Marinade: 60 min

Ingredients:

4 Salmon Steaks—4 ounces each

1 large Eggplant

Combine the following ingredients in a small bowl to make marinade:

3 Lemons—Juice only

3 Limes—Juice only

2 Tablespoons Olive Oil

1 Teaspoon Italian Seasoning

1/8 Teaspoon Hot Red Pepper Flakes

Black Pepper to taste

Directions:

1. Cut Eggplant diagonally into 1/4 inch slices.

2. Put Salmon and Eggplant into a Ziploc bag.

3. Pour marinade over Salmon and Eggplant. Seal the Ziploc bag with air removed and refrigerate for 60 minutes.

4. Oil grill and preheat to medium-high.

5. Remove Salmon from marinade.

6. Grill Salmon for 4 minutes on each side—or till Salmon flakes easily with a fork. Brush Salmon with more marinade as it cooks.

7. As Salmon cooks, add the Eggplant Slices to grill. Grill Eggplant Slices on both sides for 4 minutes, or until desired tenderness is reached.

8. Serve immediately.

Grilled

Pineapple Teriyaki Salmon

Prep: 15 min – Cook: 10 min – Serves Four – Marinade: 60 min

Ingredients:

4 Salmon Fillets—4 ounces each

1/2 Cup Teriyaki Sauce

1/2 Cup Pineapple Juice

Salt and Ground black Pepper to taste

Directions:

1. Combine Teriyaki Sauce and Pineapple Juice.

2. Marinate Salmon in Sauce for 60 minutes.

3. Oil grill and preheat to medium–high.

4. Remove Salmon from marinade.

5. Sprinkle Salmon with Salt and Ground Black Pepper to taste.

6. Grill Salmon, top side down first, for 4 minutes on each side or until salmon flakes easily with a fork. Brush Salmon with more marinade as it cooks.

7. Serve immediately.

Served With Suggestion:

White rice and grilled asparagus. Garnish Salmon with grilled pineapple slices.

1 lb. Fresh Asparagus Spears—trimmed, 1 Tablespoon Olive Oil, Salt and Black Pepper to taste. Lightly coat the Asparagus with Olive Oil, season with Salt and Black Pepper to taste. Grill for 4 to 5 minutes.

Grilled

Rosemary Dill Salmon Kebabs

Prep: 15 min – Cook: 10 min – Serves Four

Ingredients:

1 lb. Salmon Fillet – skin removed – cut into 1 inch cubes

1 Pint Cherry Tomatoes

1 Lemon—cut into 8 wedges

Combine the following ingredients in a medium bowl:

1 Tablespoon Lemon Juice

2 Teaspoons Lemon Zest

2 Tablespoon Fresh Rosemary Leaves—chopped

2 Tablespoon Fresh Dill—chopped

2 Garlic Gloves—minced

1/2 Teaspoon Kosher Salt

1/4 Teaspoon Ground Black Pepper

Directions:

1. Preheat grill to medium high.

2. Add Salmon to bowl mix, toss to coat Salmon.

3. Have eight skewers at hand. Alternate the Salmon cubes and Tomatoes on each skewer.

4. Coat grill with oil.

5. Grill the Kebabs for 3 minutes, carefully turn the Kebabs, continue to grill for another 2 to 3 minutes, or until fully cooked.

6. Serve immediately with Lemon Wedges.

Served With Suggestion:

Grilled asparagus and white rice.

1 lb. Fresh Asparagus Spears—trimmed, 1 Tablespoon Olive Oil, Salt and Black Pepper to taste. Lightly coat the Asparagus with Olive Oil, season with Salt and Black Pepper to taste. Grill for 4 to 5 minutes.

Grilled

Tomato Orange Salmon

Prep: 15 min – Cook: 10 min – Serves Four – Marinade 60 min

Ingredients:

4 Salmon Fillets—4 ounces each

Combine the following ingredients in blender to make Sauce:

2/3 Cup Tomato Ketchup

1/3 Cup Orange Juice

2 Tablespoons Orange Zest

1 Tablespoon Brown Sugar

1 Tablespoon Olive Oil

1 Tablespoon Fresh Ginger—chopped

1/4 Teaspoon Dried Nutmeg

1 Garlic Glove—chopped

Directions:

1. Mix blender contents thoroughly then transfer sauce to a bowl.

2. Brush Top of Salmon with a thick layer of sauce. Cover and refrigerate for 1 hour.

3. Oil grill and preheat to medium-high.

4. Place Salmon, top side down first, onto grill.

5. Grill Salmon 4 minutes on each side—or till Salmon flakes easily with a fork.

6. Serve immediately.

Served With Suggestion:

Baked potato and green vegetables.

Grilled

Cedar–Planked Lemon Wine Salmon

Prep: 10 min – Cook: 20 min – Serves Four – Marinade: 60 min

Ingredients:

1 Cedar plank – untreated

1 lb. Salmon Fillet

1–1/2 Cups White Wine

2 Lemons—1 juiced—1 sliced

1 Tablespoon Fresh Dill—chopped

Salt and Ground Black Pepper to taste

Directions:

1. Put the Wine, juice from 1 Lemon, and the Salmon into a ziploc bag, shake bag then squeeze out the air. Refrigerate for 60 minutes.

2. Soak Cedar plank in cold water while Salmon marinates.

3. Drain plank from water then Salmon from marinade.

4. Put Salmon – skin side down – on Cedar plank, Season Salmon with Salt and Pepper, sprinkle Dried Dill on Salmon and top with Lemon slices.

5. Put planked Salmon on your preheated 350 degree grill and cover for 20 minutes or till Salmon flakes easily with a fork.

6. Transfer cooked Salmon to serving plates.

Served With Suggestion:

Grilled zucchini, squash, eggplant and baked potato.

Slice 3/4 inch lengthwise: 3 zucchini, 3 squash and 1 eggplant. In a small bowl combine 2 tablespoons of olive oil, 2 tablespoons apple cider vinegar, 2 teaspoons Italian seasoning, 1 minced garlic clove, salt and pepper to taste. Brush vegetables with mix and grill for 5–6 minutes, or until desired tenderness is reached.

STOVE TOP RECIPES

Stove Top

Beer Battered Salmon with Dill Sauce

Prep: 20 min – Cook: 10 min – Serves Four

Ingredients:

1 lb. Salmon Fillet—skin removed—cut into 1x2 inch strips

4 Lettuce Leafs

Combine the following in a medium bowl to make the Batter:

1 Cup all-purpose Flour

1 Egg

1 Teaspoon Garlic Powder

1/4 Teaspoon Cayenne Pepper

1/4 Teaspoon Ground Black Pepper

1/4 Teaspoon Salt

1 1/4 Cups Beer

Combine the following ingredients in a small bowl to make Mustard Dill Sauce:

1 Cup Sour Cream—low fat

3 Tablespoons Fresh Dill—chopped

2 Tablespoons Onion—minced

2 Tablespoons Dijon Mustard

Salt and Pepper (to taste)

Directions:

1. Mix Mustard Dill bowl contents and put to the side.

2. Mix Beer Batter bowl contents thoroughly.

3. In a deep pan add oil to about 2 inches deep, cook on high heat till oil is hot.

4. Divide Salmon strips into 2 batches. Cook 1 batch of Salmon strips at a time. Dip Salmon strips in Beer Batter and cook in oil for 5 minutes, or until batter is golden brown.

5. Place cooked Salmon on paper towel to drain.

6. Put a Lettuce Leaf on each plate, place cooked Salmon strips on lettuce. Dribble some Mustard Dill sauce over Salmon. Serve remainder of sauce on the side.

7. Serve immediately.

STOVE TOP

Salmon with Pasta and Spicy Tomato Sauce

Prep: 15 min – Cook: 30 min – Serves Four

Ingredients:

1 lb. Salmon Fillet—skin removed—cut into 1" pieces

14.5oz. Canned Whole Tomatoes

1 lb. pack Pasta—Bow Tie

1 Onion—chopped

3 Garlic Cloves—chopped

1 Red Pepper—cubed

1 Tablespoon Olive Oil

1 Teaspoon Italian Seasoning

1/2 Teaspoon Red Pepper Flakes

1 Bay Leaf

Salt and Black Pepper to taste

Directions:

1. Drain canned Tomatoes, reserve juice. Mash Tomatoes, leaving some chunks.

2. In a saucepan add 1 tablespoon Olive Oil, add chopped Onion, cubed Red Pepper and chopped Garlic. Sauté over medium heat for 2 minutes.

3. Add Tomatoes, 1/2 of reserve Juice from Tomatoes, Italian Seasoning, Red Pepper Flakes and the Bay Leaf to saucepan. Stir well. Season with Salt and Pepper.

4. Simmer saucepan contents for 20 minutes.

5. Cook Pasta while the sauce cooks.

6. Add Salmon to the sauce, continue to cook for 4 minutes.

7. Toss the Pasta and sauce together—remove the Bay Leaf.

8. Serve immediately.

Served With Suggestion:

Serve with a green salad and whole wheat bread rolls.

Stove Top

Salmon Burger

Prep: 20 min – Cook: 10 min – Serves Four

Ingredients:

1 lb. Salmon—skin removed, chopped

1/2 Cup shredded Cheddar Cheese

1/3 Cup Breadcrumbs

1/4 Cup Red Pepper—diced

1/4 Cup Green Pepper—diced

1 Tablespoon Olive Oil

2 Tablespoons Onion—diced

1/2 Teaspoon Dijon Mustard

1/8 Teaspoon Black Pepper

1/8 Teaspoon Salt

Combine the following ingredients in a small bowl to make topping:

1/3 Cup Mayonnaise

1 Teaspoon Lemon Juice

1/3 Teaspoon dried Dill

Directions:

1. Combine all main ingredients in a bowl, mix well.

2. Divide mix into 4 equal parts and form into ½ thick Patties.

3. Add Olive Oil to a skillet.

4. Put Patties in preheated skillet—medium heat.

5. Cook Patties in skillet until golden brown on both sides—about 5 minutes each side, turning Patties over every few minutes.

6. Serve Salmon Burgers, when cooked, on a toasted bun with topping.

Served With Suggestion:

Baked potato wedges

Stove Top

Salmon Cajun Fillet

Prep: 15 min – Cook: 10 min – Serves Four

Ingredients:

4 Salmon Fillets—4 ounces each—skin removed

1 Tablespoon Olive Oil

Combine the following ingredients in a small bowl:

1–1/4 Teaspoons Paprika Pepper

1 Teaspoon Garlic Powder

1 Teaspoon Salt

1/2 Teaspoon Ground Black Pepper

1/2 Teaspoon Cayenne Pepper

1/2 Teaspoon Onion Powder

3/4 Teaspoon Dried Thyme

3/4 Teaspoon Dried Oregano

1/4 Teaspoon Red Pepper Flakes

Directions:

1. Put Olive Oil in a skillet on medium heat.

2. Rub small bowl mix on both sides of Salmon.

3. Place Salmon in skillet. Cook for 5 minutes on each side—or till Salmon flakes easily with a fork.

4. Serve immediately.

Served With Suggestion:

Serve on a whole wheat bread roll with low fat mayonnaise, lettuce, tomato and cheese with a side of potato salad or oven baked fries.

Parboil potato wedges with skin on about 10 minutes. Drain and allow cooling. Put 1 tablespoon of olive oil in a bowl; add wedges to coat with olive oil. Put potato wedges on a baking sheet, season wedges with salt and ground black pepper to taste. Bake in 425 degree preheated oven for 15–20 minutes, turning once during baking. Remove from oven and sprinkle potato wedges with apple cider vinegar.

Stove Top

Salmon Chowder

Prep: 20 min – Cook: 45 min – Serves Six

Ingredients:

12 oz. Salmon Fillet—skinless, cut into 1/2 inch cubes

3 Cups Milk—low fat

1 Cup Cream—light

1 Cup Potato—red with skin on—diced

3/4 Cup Cheddar Cheese—low fat—shredded

3/4 Cup Corn—frozen

1/2 Cup Parmesan—grated

1/2 Cup Carrots—diced

1/3 Cup Yellow Onion—chopped

1/3 Cup Celery—chopped

1 Tablespoon Olive Oil

3/4 Teaspoon Salt

1/2 Teaspoon Black Pepper

1/2 Teaspoon Dried Dill

1/2 Teaspoon Crushed Red Pepper

Directions:

1. Parboil diced Potato and Carrot for 5 minutes in same pan. Remove from heat, drain, then put Potato and Carrot to the side.

2. Melt Olive Oil in a saucepan, add chopped Onion, Sauté the Onion till partially cooked, about 2 minutes.

3. Add Milk, Cream, Frozen Corn, Celery, Salt, Black Pepper, Crushed Red Pepper and Dill to saucepan, bring to a gentle boil stirring often, reduce heat, cover and simmer for 10 minutes.

4. Next stir in the diced Potato and carrot. Simmer 10 more minutes. Add the Cheese and Salmon; continue to simmer for 5 minutes.

5. Serve immediately.

Stove Top

Salmon Club Sandwich

Prep: 15 min – Cook: 15 min – Serves Four

Ingredients:

4 Salmon Fillets—4 ounces each—skin removed

12 Slices Turkey Bacon—cooked

2 Tablespoon Olive Oil

1 Tablespoon Old Bay Seasoning

1/2 Teaspoon Black Pepper

12 Slices Whole Grain Bread—toasted

4 Lettuce Leaves

2 Large Tomatoes—cut into 12 slices

Prepare following in a small bowl:

1 Cup Mayonnaise—fat free

1/2 Teaspoon Old Bay Seasoning

Directions:

1. Put Olive Oil in a skillet on medium heat.

2. Rub Old Bay Seasoning and Black Pepper on both sides of Salmon.

3. Place Salmon in skillet. Cook for 5 minutes on each side—or till Salmon flakes easily with a fork.

4. While Salmon is cooking, Cook the Turkey Bacon and toast the Bread.

5. Spread Mayonnaise on all 12 slices of Toast.

6. Place 3 slices of Turkey Bacon on 4 slices of Toast.

7. Cover Turkey Bacon with a Lettuce Leaf and 3 slices of Tomato.

8. Put slice of Toast, Mayonnaise side down, on top of Tomato.

9. Put Salmon Fillet on top of 2nd slice of Toast.

10. Cover Salmon Fillet with 3rd slice of Toast, Mayonnaise side facing down.

11. Cut Club Sandwich diagonally and serve.

Stove Top

Cream of Salmon Soup

Prep: 20 min – Cook: 25 min – Serves Six

Ingredients:

1-1/2 lbs. Salmon Fillet—skin removed

4 Cups Milk—low fat

2 Cups Water

1/4 Cup All-purpose Flour

1 Onion—diced

1 Celery Stalk—diced

2 Teaspoons Salt

1 Teaspoon Dried Parsley

1/2 Teaspoon Dried Dill

Ground Black Pepper to taste

Directions:

1. Cut the Salmon into strips and grind in a blender.

2. Bring to the boil 2 cups of Water in a saucepan. Add the blended Salmon, simmer till cooked. Then add the Onion, Celery, Parsley and Dill. Remove from heat.

3. In another saucepan combine the Milk and Flour, cook on low heat till Milk thickens, stirring constantly. Add the Butter and Salt. Remove from heat.

4. Gradually add Milk saucepan contents to the Salmon saucepan. Cook over medium–low heat till thick and smooth, stirring constantly.

5. Season with Black Ground Pepper.

6. Serve immediately.

Served With Suggestion:

Garnish soup with fresh Parsley. A green salad and whole wheat bread Roll.

Stove Top

Salmon Fettuccini Alfredo

Prep: 10 min – Cook: 20 min – Serves Four

Ingredients:

1 lb. Salmon Fillet— skin removed—cut into 1" pieces

1 lb. Fettuccini

1-1/2 Cups Milk—low fat

1 Cup Cherry Tomatoes

3/4 Cup Parmesan—grated

1/2 Cup Mozzarella Cheese—shredded

1 Tablespoon Lemon juice

2 Teaspoons Flour

1 Teaspoon Dried Parsley

1/2 Teaspoon Dried Dill

1/4 Teaspoon Dry Mustard

Salt and Black Pepper to taste

Directions:

1. Cook the Fettuccini per package instructions.

2. Put Milk and Flour in a saucepan, mix well. Add Parsley, Dill and Mustard, stir well.

3. Cook over medium heat for 5 minutes, stirring often.

4. Stir Parmesan and Mozzarella Cheese into saucepan, lower heat, cook till sauce thickens.

5. When sauce has thickened add the Cherry Tomatoes, Salmon and Lemon Juice. Continue to cook for 4–5 minutes or until Salmon flakes easily with a fork.

6. Season sauce with Salt and Pepper to taste.

7. Toss the Pasta and Sauce.

8. Serve immediately.

Served With Suggestion:

A side salad and whole wheat bread rolls or garlic bread completes this delicious meal.

Stove Top

Salmon Fried Potato Nugget Salad

Prep: 20 min – Cook: 20 min – Serves Four

Ingredients:

1 lb. Salmon Fillet—chopped—skin removed

1 lb. Potatoes—mashed

1/2 Cup All-purpose Flour

1 Tablespoon Olive Oil

Salt and Ground Black Pepper to taste

Lettuce—shredded

4 Tomatoes—cut into wedges

Combine the following ingredients in a medium bowl:

1/2 Cup Cheddar Cheese—shredded

2 Eggs

2 Tablespoons Shallots—minced

1 Tablespoon Fresh Parsley—chopped

1 Tablespoon Fresh Dill—chopped

Sauce: 1/2 Cup Mayonnaise, 1/4 Cup Lemon Juice, 1 Tablespoon Fresh Dill—chopped

Directions:

1. Peel and boil the Potato, mash when cooked.

2. Add mashed Potato to medium bowl mix, mix well. Set to the side.

3. Make Sauce, put to the side.

4. Put 1 Tablespoon Olive Oil and chopped Salmon in a skillet, cook over medium–high heat for 4 minutes, or until Salmon is cooked.

5. Combine cooked Salmon with Potato mix. Season the mix with Salt and Pepper. Form mix into 1-inch nuggets, and dip nuggets in flour.

6. Deep fry nuggets in vegetable oil for 2–3 minutes.

7. Put Lettuce on serving plates; add nuggets on top of lettuce. Garnish with Tomato and serve with sauce.

8. Serve immediately.

Served With Suggestion:

Add red onion and cucumber to the salad. Serve with whole wheat rolls.

Stove Top

Paprika Salmon and Chili Beans

Prep: 10 min – Cook: 25 min – Serves Four

Ingredients:

4 Salmon Fillets—4 ounces each—skin removed

2 Cans Beans in Chili Sauce

1 Red Pepper—cubed

1 Green Pepper—Cubed

3 Tablespoons Flour

3 Tablespoons Olive Oil

1 Tablespoon Parsley—fresh—chopped

1 Teaspoon Paprika

Salt and Black Pepper to taste

Directions:

1. Combine the Flour, Paprika, Salt and Pepper in a bowl. Coat both sides of Salmon with mix.

2. Put 1 Tablespoon of Olive Oil in a skillet over medium heat.

3. Place Salmon Fillets in skillet. Cook for 5 minutes on each side—or until Salmon flakes easily with a fork.

4. Remove Salmon and put to the side.

5. In the same skillet add 2 Tablespoons of Olive Oil. Add the Red and Green cubed Peppers, cook for 3 minutes.

6. Add the Beans in Chili Sauce to skillet. Cook for 5 minutes, stirring often. Remove from heat, add chopped Parsley.

7. Put the Beans onto plates and top with Salmon Fillet.

8. Serve immediately.

Served With Suggestion:

A green salad and whole wheat bread rolls make this meal complete.

Stove Top

Chili Salmon Patties with Lime Dressing

Prep: 20 min – Cook: 10 min – Serves Four

Ingredients:

1 lb. Salmon Fillet—skin removed—chopped

2 16oz Cans Chickpeas

2 Onions—chopped

3 Red Chilies—seeds removed—chopped

6 Garlic Cloves—chopped

1/2 cup Cilantro—finely chopped

1 Egg

2 Tablespoons Olive Oil

1 Teaspoon Fresh Ginger—chopped

Salt and Black Pepper to taste

Combine the following ingredients in a small bowl to make Lime Dressing:

1 Cup Mayonnaise

3 Limes—juiced

1/4 Cup Fresh Parsley—chopped

2 Garlic Gloves—minced

Directions:

1. Put 1 tablespoon of Olive Oil in a skillet over medium heat; add Garlic, Onion, Chili, Ginger and Salmon to skillet, sauté till cooked, about 4 minutes.

2. Put the cooked skillet contents, Chickpeas and Egg into a blender. Blend the ingredients. Put to side and allow cooling for 15 minutes.

3. When mix has cooled, shape into medium size patties, refrigerate patties for 15 minutes.

4. Make Lime dressing and refrigerate.

5. Put 1 tablespoon of Olive Oil in a skillet over medium heat; fry patties till browned – about 3 minutes on each side.

6. Allow cooked patties to drain on paper towel for a few minutes before serving.

7. Top patties with a spoonful of Lime dressing and Serve immediately.

Stove Top

Salmon Quesadillas

Prep: 15 min – Cook: 10 min – Serves Four

Ingredients:

1 lb. Salmon—skinless—chopped

8oz Mexican Blend Cheese—low fat—shredded

2 Tomatoes—diced

1 Tablespoon Olive Oil

1 Tablespoon Butter—softened

2 Teaspoons Lemon Juice

2 Teaspoons Basil—dried

2 Garlic Cloves—minced

1/2 Teaspoon Black Pepper

1/8 Teaspoon Salt

4 Flour Tortillas—10 inches

Directions:

1. Put Olive Oil in a skillet over medium heat; add Garlic and Salmon to skillet, sauté till cooked, about 4 minutes.

2. Add Basil, Salt, Pepper and Lemon Juice to skillet, stir well, then remove from heat. Put skillet contents into a bowl.

3. Spread Butter on one side of each Tortilla. Place Tortilla Butter side down in skillet.

4. Cover 1/2 of Tortilla with 1/2 cup of Salmon; sprinkle Salmon with diced Tomato and 2oz of Cheese. Fold Tortilla in half.

5. Cook in skillet on medium to low heat for 2 minutes, flip over Tortilla and cook another 2 minutes, or until Tortilla begins to brown. Repeat process for the other 3 Tortillas.

6. Serve immediately.

Stove Top

Salmon Scrambled Eggs

Prep: 10 min – Cook: 10 min – Serves Four

Ingredients:

1 Salmon Fillet—8 ounces—skin removed—chopped

1/2 Cup Cherry Tomatoes—cut tomatoes in half

1/3 Cup Red Onion—chopped

1-1/2 Tablespoon Olive Oil

Fresh Basil Leaves—for garnish

Combine the following ingredients in a medium bowl:

6 Eggs

1/3 Cup Cheddar Cheese—low fat—shredded

1 Tablespoon Milk

1/4 Teaspoon Dried Basil

1/4 Teaspoon Cayenne Pepper

Pinch of Salt

Directions:

1. Heat 1 Tablespoon Olive Oil in a skillet on medium-high heat; add chopped Salmon and Onion, sauté till done–about 4 minutes. Salmon will flake as it cooks.

2. Add bowl mix to skillet, turn down heat to medium. Continue cooking stirring constantly till Eggs are cooked. Remove from heat; put Scrambled Eggs on serving plates.

3. Add 1/2 Tablespoon Olive Oil and Cherry Tomatoes to same skillet and cook Cherry Tomatoes about 2 minutes on medium-high heat.

4. Garnish Scrambled Egg with Tomatoes and Fresh Basil leaves.

5. Serve immediately.

Served With Suggestion:

Whole wheat toast or Bagel with low fat cream cheese.

Stove Top

Salmon Stir Fry

Prep: 20 min – Cook: 20 min – Serves Four – Marinade: 60 min

Ingredients:

1 lb. Salmon Fillet—skin removed—cut into 1" cubes

1 1/2 Cups Stir-fry Sauce

3 Carrots—sliced thin

1 Red Pepper—cut into strips

3/4 Cup Green Beans

1/2 Cup Orange Juice

1/2 Head of Broccoli—cut to small florets

4 Scallions—chopped

1/3 Cup Cilantro—chopped

3 Tablespoons Peanut Oil

2 Tablespoons Fresh ginger—grated

1 Garlic Clove—crushed

1 Teaspoon Sesame Oil

Salt and Black Pepper to taste

1 Orange—for garnish

Directions:

1. Heat Wok over medium-high heat.

2. Add Peanut Oil, Ginger, Garlic and Scallions to Wok. Cook for 1 minute.

3. Add Red Pepper, Green Beans, Carrots and Broccoli. Sauté for 5 minutes.

4. Add Stir-fry Sauce and Salmon, continue to cook for 4 minutes, and then add Orange Juice, Cilantro and Sesame Oil. Remove from heat.

5. Season to taste with Salt and Black Pepper.

6 Cut Orange into wedges for garnish.

7. Serve immediately.

Served With Suggestion:

Serve over a bed of brown or white rice.

Stove Top

Thai Coconut Curried Salmon

Prep: 20 min – Cook: 20 min – Serves Four

Ingredients:

1 lb. Salmon Fillet—skin removed—cubed

2 Cups Coconut Milk—low fat

1 Cup Chicken Stock—low sodium

1 Cup Green Beans

1 Cup Onion—sliced thin

1/2 Cup Fresh Basil Leaves—chopped

2 Tablespoons Lime Juice

1 Tablespoon Soy Sauce

1 Tablespoon Olive Oil

1 Tablespoon Sugar

1 Tablespoon Fresh Ginger—minced

2 Teaspoons Curry Powder

1 Teaspoon Red Curry Paste

2 Garlic Cloves—Chopped

Salt and Ground Black Pepper to taste

Directions:

1. In a large saucepan, sauté Onion with Olive Oil and Curry Powder for 3 minutes over medium-high heat.

2. Add the following ingredients to saucepan: Coconut Milk, Chicken Stock, Lime Juice, Soy Sauce, Sugar, Ginger, Curry Paste and Garlic. Bring to a boil then reduce heat to simmer.

3. Add cubed Salmon, cover and simmer for 5 minutes, then add Green Beans. Simmer for another 4 minutes or until Salmon flakes easily with a fork.

4. Season with Salt and Ground Black Pepper to taste.

5. Serve immediately.

Served With Suggestion:

This can be served over rice, or served as a soup. Garnish with Basil Leaves.

Stove Top

Salmon with Tomato Tarragon Wine Sauce

Prep: 20 min – Cook: 20 min – Serves Four

Ingredients:

4 Salmon Fillets—4 ounces each—skin removed

1 Cup Milk—Low Fat

1/2 Cup Cherry Tomatoes—cut into halves

2 Tablespoons Butter

2 Tablespoons Dry White Wine

2 Tablespoons Half and Half

1 Tablespoon All-purpose Flour

1 Tablespoon Shallots—minced

1 Teaspoon Dried Tarragon

Salt and Ground Black Pepper

Directions:

1. Lightly coat baking dish with cooking spray.

2. Place Salmon in baking dish. Lightly season Salmon with Salt and Ground Black Pepper.

3. Put baking dish in preheated 400 degree oven for 20 minutes or till Salmon flakes easily with a fork.

4. Melt the Butter in a saucepan over medium heat; add the Shallots and sauté for 2 minutes then stir in the Flour. Remove saucepan from heat.

5. Add the Milk to saucepan, stirring well, return saucepan to medium heat, stirring constantly till sauce thickens.

6. Lower heat to medium-low and stir in the Wine, Half and Half, Tarragon and Tomatoes. Cook for 2 minutes, then season with Salt and Ground Black Pepper to taste.

7. Spoon the Sauce over the Salmon.

8. Serve immediately.

Served With Suggestion:

Brown rice and your favorite green vegetable compliment this Salmon and Sauce dish.

Stove Top

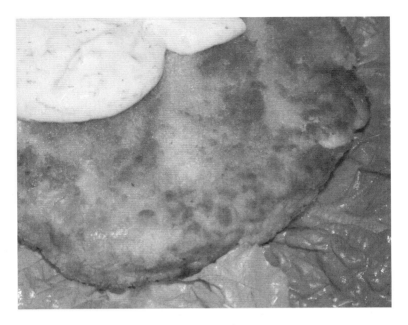

Salmon Cakes

Prep: 20 min – Set: 45 min – Cook: 20 min – Serves Four

Ingredients:

8 oz. Salmon Fillet—skin removed—cut into 1" cubes

1/4 Cup Pineapple Juice

1/4 Cup Lemon Juice

2 Tablespoon All-purpose Flour

1 Tablespoon Olive Oil

Combine the following ingredients in a medium bowl:

1 lb. Potatoes—mashed

1/4 Cup Cheddar Cheese—shredded—low fat

1 Egg—raw

1/4 Teaspoon Dried Dill

1/4 Teaspoon Dried Parsley

1/2 Teaspoon Old Bay Seasoning

Salt and Ground Black Pepper to Taste

Coating: 1/4 Cup Bread Crumbs, 1 Egg–beaten, 1/4 Cup Flour

Topping: 1/4 Cup Mayonnaise, 2 Teaspoons Lemon Juice, 1/2 Teaspoon Dried Dill

Directions:

1. Combine Salmon cubes with the Pineapple and Lemon Juice in a bowl. Put bowl in refrigerator to marinate.

2. Make mashed Potato. Combine medium bowl mix, stir well.

3. Remove Salmon from juice, discard the juice.

4. Add Olive Oil and Salmon to skillet over medium heat, cook 4 minutes, stirring often. Salmon will flake.

5. Add the cooked Salmon to Potato, mix well. Place the Mixture in the refrigerator for 45 minutes in order to cool.

6. Combine the Topping ingredients and put in refrigerator.

7. Divide the mix into 4 equal parts and form into 1/2 thick patties.

8. Coat the Cakes with Flour, dip each Cake into Egg, and then coat Cakes with Breadcrumbs.

9. Add Olive Oil to a large skillet; cook Cakes over medium–high heat, till Cakes are golden brown—about 4 minutes each side.

10. Serve immediately with Topping on each Cake.

Served With Suggestion:

A green salad and whole wheat bread rolls.

ABOUT THE AUTHOR

Thank you for reading, and thank you for your support.

I hope you enjoy these wonderful healthy recipes as much as my family and friends. Salmon is part of my family's weekly diet and with so many cooking options this healthy fish can become a tasty addition to yours. Together we can help reduce the predicted 51% obese rate in the USA set to occur in 2030. Please encourage your family and friends to eat healthier.

Best regards, Colin.

Coming soon: **CHICKEN a cookbook** – easy to cook healthy recipes in 30 minutes and less. Find it on Amazon.com.

Made in the USA
San Bernardino, CA
04 February 2015